INGLÉS
DICCIONARIO VISUAL

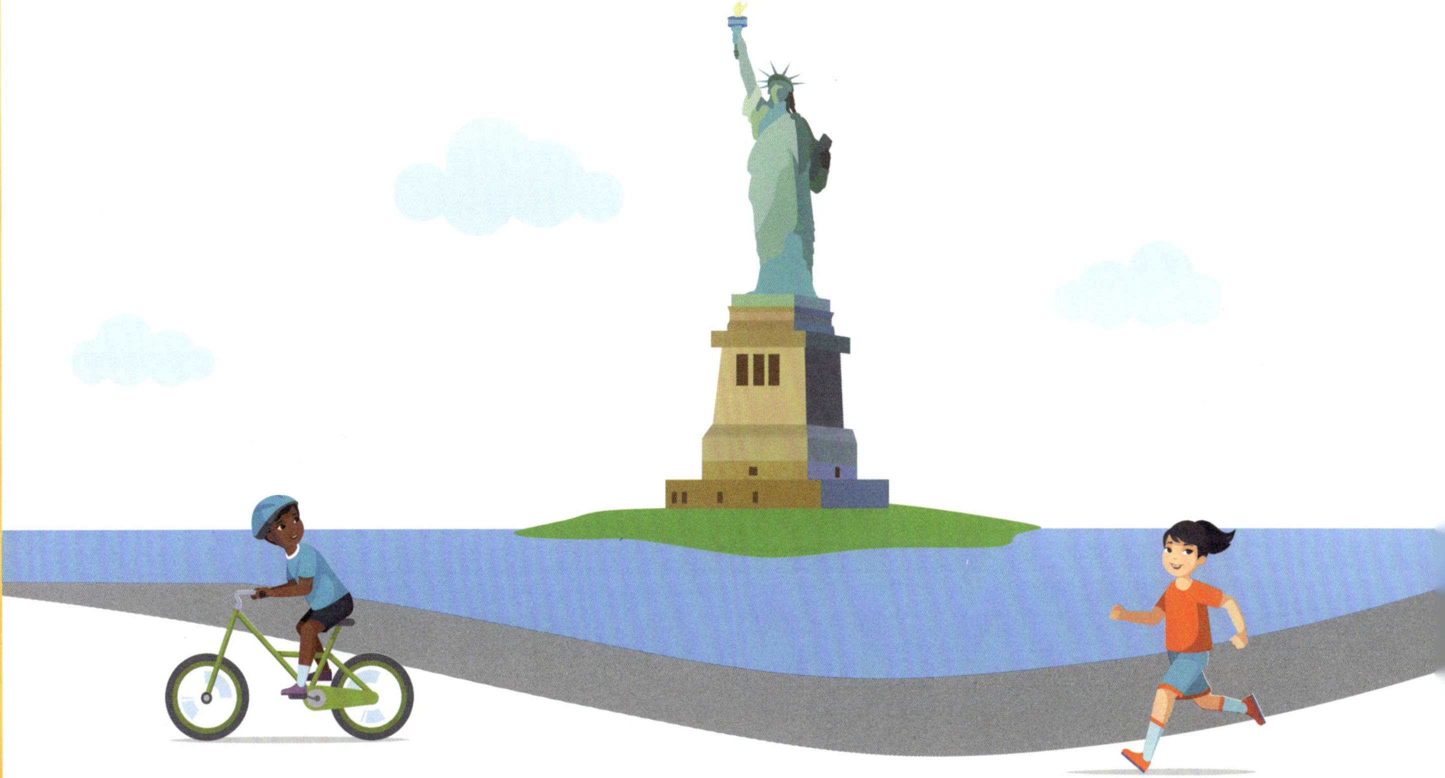

© 2024 Rosetta Stone, LLC, una filial de IXL Learning, Inc. Todos los derechos reservados. Ninguna parte de esta publicación puede ser reproducida, almacenada en un sistema de recuperación o transmitida, en ninguna forma o por ningún medio (electrónico, mecánico, fotocopiado, grabado o de otra manera) sin el permiso previo por escrito de IXL Learning.

© 2024 Rosetta Stone, LLC, a subsidiary of IXL Learning, Inc. All rights reserved. No part of this publication may be reproduced, stored in a retrieval system, or transmitted, in any form or by any means (electronic, mechanical, photocopying, recording, or otherwise) without the prior written permission of IXL Learning.

ISBN: 978-1-947569-87-4

28 27 26 25 24 1 2 3 4 5

Impreso en China

Printed in China

Acerca de este libro

¿Quieres aprender algunas palabras en inglés? Antes de comenzar, aquí tienes información útil para ayudarte a aprovechar este libro al máximo.

Inglés estadounidense

El inglés se habla en muchos países de todo el mundo. En este libro utilizamos el inglés estadounidense. Aprenderás palabras utilizadas por la mayoría de los hablantes de los Estados Unidos. En otros lugares donde se habla inglés se podrían escribir y pronunciar dichas palabras de forma diferente. ¡Incluso se podrían usar otras completamente distintas para las cosas que ves en este diccionario!

Vocales y consonantes en inglés

El alfabeto en inglés tiene las mismas letras que el alfabeto en español, excepto la *ñ*. Y al igual que en español, el inglés tiene cinco vocales escritas: **a**, **e**, **i**, **o** y **u**. (A veces, la **y** también se considera una vocal en inglés.) Pero, ¡cuidado! Las vocales en inglés normalmente no se pronuncian como las vocales en español. Por ejemplo, la **a** en **cake** se pronuncia EY.

Notarás que algunas consonantes en inglés se pronuncian como las consonantes en español. Por ejemplo, las letras **b**, **f**, **l**, **m**, **n** y **s** suenan prácticamente igual en inglés y en español. Pero también hay diferencias importantes a tener en cuenta.

Cuando veas que una palabra comienza con **h** más vocal en inglés, pronuncia la **h** como la *x* de *México*. Por ejemplo, **hen** se pronuncia HEHN.

Cuando veas la combinación de letras **ll**, no la pronuncies como lo haces en español. Pronúnciala como si fuera una sola **l**. Por ejemplo, **yellow** se pronuncia YEH-lo.

En inglés, la **r** no se pronuncia como la *r* en español. En español, se toca el paladar con la lengua cuando se pronuncia la *r*. Para decir la **r** en inglés estadounidense, se acerca la lengua al paladar sin tocarlo.

Pronunciar palabras en inglés

La mejor manera de aprender a decir las palabras en inglés es escucharlas pronunciadas por un hablante nativo de inglés. Escanea los códigos QR del libro para escuchar cada palabra.

Debajo de cada palabra en inglés en este libro, encontrarás una guía sobre cómo decir la palabra.

Datos curiosos

A lo largo de este libro compartimos datos curiosos y útiles sobre las palabras en inglés que estás aprendiendo.

Índice

Numbers (Números)

NUHM-buhrz

0

zero
ZI-ro
cero

1

one
wuhn
uno

2

two
tu
dos

3

three
thri
tres

4

four
for
cuatro

5

five
fayv
cinco

6

six
sihks
seis

7

seven
SEH-vihn
siete

8

eight
eyt
ocho

9

nine
nayn
nueve

10

ten
tehn
diez

11

eleven
uh-LEH-vihn
once

12
twelve
twehlv
doce

13
thirteen
thuhr-TIN
trece

14
fourteen
for-TIN
catorce

15
fifteen
fihf-TIN
quince

DATO CURIOSO:
La palabra **teenager** (o su diminutivo, **teen**) se refiere a una persona de entre trece y diecinueve años. ¿Sabes por qué? Pista: observa las terminaciones de todas las palabras entre **thirteen** (*trece*) y **nineteen** (*diecinueve*).

16
sixteen
sihks-TIN
dieciséis

17
seventeen
seh-vuhn-TIN
diecisiete

18
eighteen
ey-TIN
dieciocho

19
nineteen
nayn-TIN
diecinueve

Numbers (Números)

NUHM-buhrz

20

twenty

TWUHN-i

veinte

30

thirty

THUHR-di

treinta

40

forty

FOR-di

cuarenta

50

fifty

FIHF-di

cincuenta

60

sixty

SIHKS-di

sesenta

70

seventy

SEH-vuhn-di

setenta

80

eighty

EY-di

ochenta

90

ninety

NAYN-di

noventa

100

one hundred

wuhn HUHN-drihd

cien

Colors (Colores)

KUH-luhrz

red
rehd
rojo

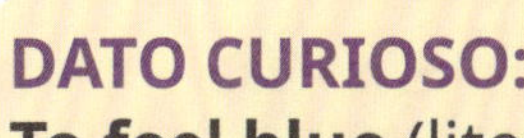

blue
blu
azul

DATO CURIOSO:
To feel blue (literalmente, *sentirse azul*) es una expresión que significa 'sentirse triste'. En español hay expresiones equivalentes, tales como *estar agüitado, estar de capa caída* y *tener el ánimo por los suelos.*

yellow
YEH-lo
amarillo

green
grin
verde

purple
PUHR-puhl
morado

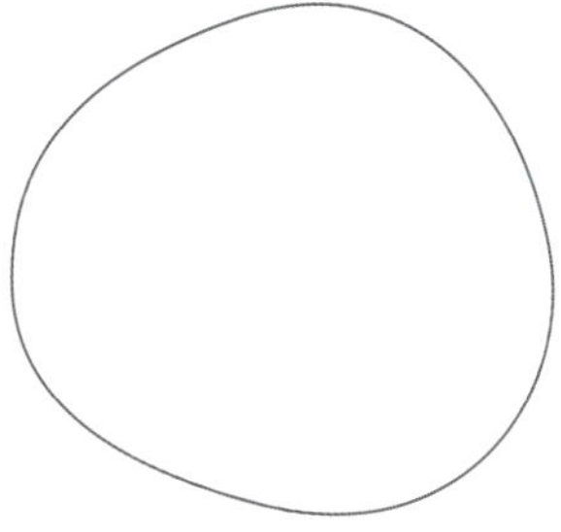

white
wayt
blanco

¡Lleva tus habilidades en inglés al siguiente nivel!

Regístrate en RosettaStone.com.

¡Escanea este código QR para escuchar las palabras!

Colors (Colores)

KUH-luhrz

black
blahk
negro

brown
braun
café

orange
OR-ihnj
anaranjado

pink
pihngk
rosa

gray
grey
gris

DATO CURIOSO:
Orange se refiere tanto al color (*anaranjado* o *naranja*) como a la fruta (*naranja*).

DATO CURIOSO:
Se puede usar **light** y **dark** para describir colores *claros* y *oscuros*. La palabra **light** también puede significar 'liviano, ligero'.

light blue
layt blu
azul claro

dark blue
dark blu
azul oscuro

Shapes (Figuras)

sheyps

square
skwehr
cuadrado

rectangle
REHK-teyng-guhl
rectángulo

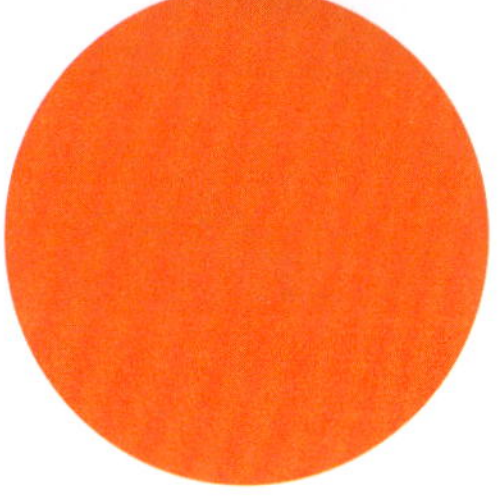

circle
SUHR-kuhl
círculo

oval
O-vuhl
óvalo

triangle
TRAY-ahng-guhl
triángulo

diamond
DAY-mihnd
rombo

star
star
estrella

heart
hart
corazón

hexagon
HEHK-suh-gan
hexágono

Animals (Animales)

AHN-ih-muhlz

cat
kaht
gato

dog
dag
perro

bird
buhrd
pájaro

rabbit
RAH-biht
conejo

hamster
HAHM-stuhr
hámster

cow
kau
vaca

horse
hors
caballo

goat
got
cabra

pig
pihg
cerdo

sheep
ship
oveja

duck
duhk
pato

hen
hehn
gallina

rooster
RU-stuhr
gallo

goose
gus
ganso

turkey
TUHR-ki
pavo

fox
faks
zorro

Animals (Animales)
AHN-ih-muhlz

frog
frag
rana

mouse
maus
ratón

bear
behr
oso

snake
sneyk
serpiente

DATO CURIOSO:
¡Cuidado! La palabra **deer** suena igual que la palabra **dear**, que significa 'querido'.

deer
dihr
venado

owl
aul
búho

squirrel
skwuhrl
ardilla

skunk
skuhngk
zorrillo

raccoon

rah-KUN

mapache

hedgehog

HEHJ-hag

erizo

turtle

TUHR-duhl

tortuga

mole

mol

topo

DATO CURIOSO:
Al igual que *topo*, ¡la palabra **mole** también puede referirse a un espía infiltrado!

wolf

woolf

lobo

zebra

ZI-bruh

cebra

elephant

EH-lih-fihnt

elefante

lion

LAY-ihn

león

Animals (Animales)

AHN-ih-muhlz

monkey
MUHNG-ki

mono

gorilla
guh-RIH-luh

gorila

rhinoceros
ray-NA-suhr-ihs

rinoceronte

giraffe
jih-RAHF

jirafa

hippopotamus
hih-po-PA-duh-mihs

hipopótamo

DATO CURIOSO: **Hippopotamus** y **rhinoceros** a menudo se acortan a **hippo** y **rhino**.

flamingo
fluh-MIHNG-go

flamenco

tiger
TAY-guhr

tigre

koala
ko-A-luh

koala

parrot
PEH-riht
loro

DATO CURIOSO:
El verbo **to parrot** significa 'repetir mecánicamente lo que alguien dice', como *repetir como un loro*.

crocodile
KRA-kuh-dayl
cocodrilo

bat
baht
murciélago

panda
PAHN-duh
panda

camel
KAH-muhl
camello

kangaroo
kahng-guh-RU
canguro

penguin
PEYNG-gwihn
pingüino

whale
weyl
ballena

Animals (Animales)

AHN-ih-muhlz

dolphin
DAL-fihn
delfín

shark
shark
tiburón

crab
krahb
cangrejo

fish
fihsh
pez

DATO CURIOSO:
Alguien descrito como **a fish out of water** está en una situación incómoda o totalmente desconocida. Más o menos es lo opuesto a decir que está *como pez en el agua* o *en su elemento*.

lobster
LAB-stuhr
langosta

sea star
si star
estrella de mar

seal
sil
foca

octopus
AK-tuh-puhs
pulpo

seahorse
SI-hors
caballito de mar

fly
flay
mosca

bee
bi
abeja

spider
SPAY-duhr
araña

moth
math
polilla

caterpillar
KAH-duhr-pih-luhr
oruga

DATO CURIOSO:
Si tienes **butterflies in your stomach**, significa que te sientes nervioso por algo. En español se puede usar la expresión equivalente *tener mariposas en el estómago.*

butterfly
BUH-duhr-flay
mariposa

Animals (Animales)
AHN-ih-muhlz

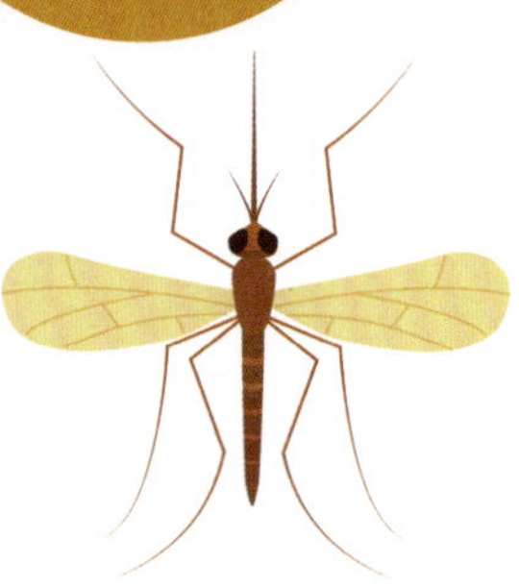

mosquito
muh-SKI-do
mosquito

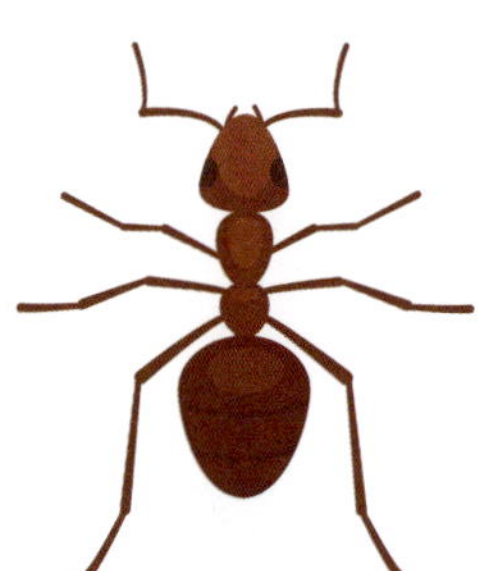

ant
ahnt
hormiga

centipede
SEHN-tih-pid
ciempiés

firefly
FAY-uhr-flay
luciérnaga

grasshopper
GRAHS-ha-puhr
saltamontes

beetle
BI-duhl
escarabajo

worm
wuhrm
gusano

DATO CURIOSO:
To open a can of worms significa 'crear muchos problemas nuevos al intentar resolver uno concreto'. Es similar a la expresión *abrir la caja de Pandora*, que también existe en inglés (**to open Pandora's box**).

dragonfly
DRAH-gihn-flay
libélula

Fruits and vegetables
(Frutas y verduras)
fruts ahnd VEHJ-tuh-buhlz

apple
AH-puhl
manzana

DATO CURIOSO:
Mientras que en español se usa la frase *comparar peras con manzanas* para comparar dos cosas muy distintas, en inglés se usa la frase **compare apples and oranges** (literalmente, *comparar manzanas con naranjas*.)

orange
OR-ihnj
naranja

banana
buh-NAH-nuh
plátano

strawberry
STRA-beh-ri
fresa

blueberry
BLU-beh-ri
arándano azul

cranberry
KRAHN-behr-i
arándano rojo

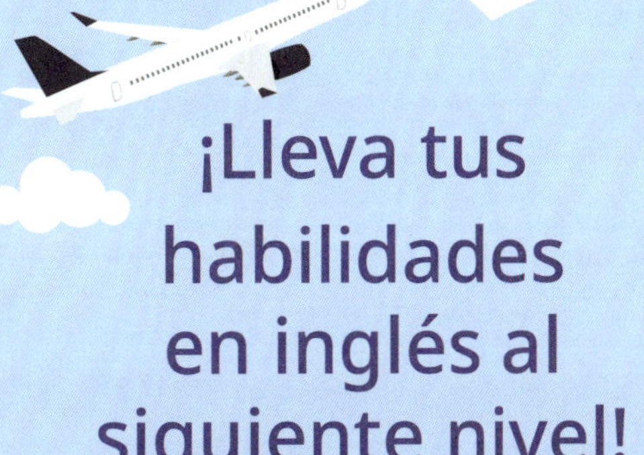

¡Lleva tus habilidades en inglés al siguiente nivel!

Regístrate en RosettaStone.com.

Fruits and vegetables
(Frutas y verduras)
fruts ahnd VEHJ-tuh-buhlz

grapefruit
GREYP-frut
toronja

DATO CURIOSO:
La palabra **grapefruit** en inglés se compone de dos palabras: **grape** (*uva*) y **fruit** (*fruta*). Esto puede ser porque las toronjas crecen en racimos como las uvas.

peach
pich
durazno

melon
MEH-lihn
melón

watermelon
WA-duhr-mehl-uhn
sandía

DATO CURIOSO:
La palabra **watermelon** en inglés se compone de dos palabras: **water** (*agua*) y **melon** (*melón*), lo cual tiene sentido, ya que las sandías contienen principalmente agua.

pineapple
PAYN-ah-puhl
piña

pear
pehr
pera

lime
laym
limón

lemon
LEH-mihn
lima

blackberry
BLAHK-beh-ri
zarzamora

raspberry
RAHZ-beh-ri
frambuesa

cherry
CHEH-ri
cereza

DATO CURIOSO:
Si algo se describe como **the cherry on top** (literalmente, *la cereza encima*), significa que es el toque final que hace que algo bueno sea aún mejor, o incluso perfecto. Es similar a la expresión *la cereza del pastel*.

DATO CURIOSO:
Un **kiwi** también es un pequeño pájaro no volador que habita solo en Nueva Zelanda.

kiwi
KI-wi
kiwi

apricot
AH-prih-kat
chabacano

Fruits and vegetables
(Frutas y verduras)
fruts ahnd VEHJ-tuh-buhlz

mango
MAHNG-go
mango

papaya
puh-PAY-yuh
papaya

guava
GWA-vuh
guayaba

passion fruit
PAH-shihn frut
maracuyá

plum
pluhm
ciruela

prune
prun
ciruela pasa

grapes
greyps
uvas

raisins
REY-zihnz
pasas

DATO CURIOSO:
¿Sabías que una pasa es una uva seca? La palabra inglesa **raisin** viene de *raisin*, palabra francesa que significa 'uva'.

fig
fihg
higo

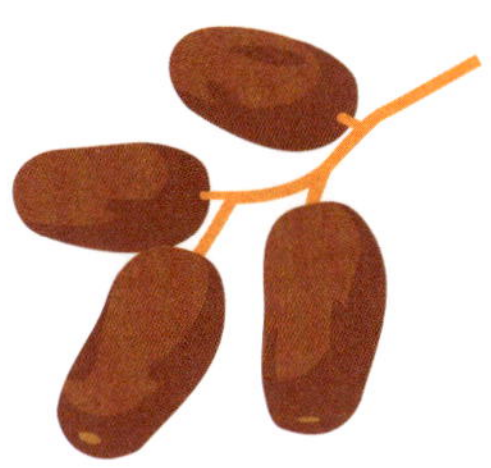

date
deyt
dátil

persimmon
puhr-SIH-mihn
caqui

coconut
KO-kuh-nuht
coco

zucchini
zu-KI-ni
calabacita

olive
A-lihv
aceituna

carrot
KEH-riht
zanahoria

bell pepper
behl PEH-puhr
pimiento

Fruits and vegetables
(Frutas y verduras)
fruts ahnd VEHJ-tuh-buhlz

broccoli
BRA-kuh-li

brócoli

cucumber
KYU-kuhm-buhr

pepino

DATO CURIOSO:
Una persona que es **cool as a cucumber** (literalmente, *fresco como un pepino*) es capaz de mantenerse calmada, incluso cuando está bajo presión.

spinach
SPIH-nihch

espinacas

onion
UHN-yihn

cebolla

tomato
tuh-MEY-do

tomate

DATO CURIOSO:
En lugar de **eggplant**, algunos países de habla inglesa usan el término **aubergine**, que se parece más al español *berenjena*.

eggplant
EHG-plahnt

berenjena

lettuce
LEH-dihs

lechuga

DATO CURIOSO:
Si se describe a dos personas como **two peas in a pod** (literalmente, *dos chícharos en una vaina*), significa que son muy similares. En español se dice que dos personas son *como dos gotas de agua*.

peas
piz
chícharos

cabbage
KAH-bihj
col

cauliflower
KA-luh-flau-uhr
coliflor

potato
puh-TEY-do
papa

sweet potato
swit puh-TEY-do
camote

DATO CURIOSO:
La palabra **sweet potato** se puede traducir literalmente como *papa dulce*. En realidad, ¡las papas y los camotes son parientes lejanos!

Brussels sprouts
BRUH-suhl sprauts
coles de Bruselas

Fruits and vegetables
(Frutas y verduras)
fruts ahnd VEHJ-tuh-buhlz

pumpkin
PUHMP-kihn
calabaza

parsnip
PAR-snihp
zanahoria blanca

kale
keyl
col rizada

green beans
grin binz
ejotes

artichoke
AR-dih-chok
alcachofa

radish
RAH-dihsh
rábano

avocado
a-vuh-KA-do
aguacate

DATO CURIOSO:
¿Te diste cuenta de que **avocado** suena muy parecido a *aguacate*? ¡La palabra inglesa de hecho viene del español!

asparagus
uh-SPEH-rih-gihs
espárrago

DATO CURIOSO:
¡Cuidado! No confundas **leek** (*puerro*) con **leak** (*gotear*), aunque se pronuncien igual.

leek
lik
puerro

celery
SEH-luh-ri
apio

mushroom
MUHSH-rum
champiñón

garlic
GAR-lihk
ajo

shallot
SHAH-liht
chalote

DATO CURIOSO:
Otra palabra para **corn** es **maize**, parecida a la española *maíz*.

corn
korn
maíz

ginger
JIHN-juhr
jengibre

¡Escanea este código QR para escuchar las palabras!

Nuts (Frutos secos)

nuhts

walnut
WAL-nuht

nuez

hazelnut
HEY-zuhl-nuht

avellana

pistachio
pih-STAH-shi-o

pistacho

peanut
PI-nuht

cacahuate

almond
AL-mihnd

almendra

cashew
KAH-shu

nuez de la India

pecan
pih-KAN

nuez pecana

DATO CURIOSO:
¡La palabra **pecan** se puede pronunciar de varias maneras en los EE. UU.! Por ejemplo, algunas personas ponen el énfasis en la segunda sílaba (pih-KAN), mientras otras ponen el énfasis en la primera sílaba (PI-kahn).

chestnut
CHEHS-nuht

castaña

Food (Comida)

fud

egg
ehg
huevo

butter
BUH-duhr
mantequilla

yogurt
YO-guhrt
yogur

jam
jahm
mermelada

honey
HUH-ni
miel

bread
brehd
pan

cereal
SIR-i-uhl
cereales

oatmeal
OT-mil
avena

DATO CURIOSO:
En el Reino Unido, la palabra **porridge** suele usarse en lugar de **oatmeal**, que es propia de Estados Unidos.

Food (Comida)
fud

sandwich
SAHND-wihch
sándwich

DATO CURIOSO:
El **sandwich** recibe su nombre en honor al cuarto conde de Sandwich, un aristócrata británico del siglo XVIII. Según la leyenda, el conde de Sandwich a menudo solicitaba lonchas de carne entre dos rebanadas de pan, lo que le permitía comer sin interrumpir sus juegos de cartas o su trabajo.

salad
SAH-luhd
ensalada

soup
sup
sopa

cheese
chiz
queso

pasta
PA-stuh
pasta

noodles
NU-duhlz
fideos

DATO CURIOSO:
Cuando te están tomando una foto, te podrían decir "**Say cheese!**" (literalmente, *¡Di queso!*) para que sonrías, que sería lo mismo que decir *¡Patata!* en España.

rice
rays
arroz

soybean
SOY-bin
soya

lentils
LEHN-tuhls
lentejas

beans
binz
frijoles

DATO CURIOSO:
La expresión **to spill the beans** (literalmente, *derramar los frijoles*) significa 'revelar un secreto', algo similar a *soltar la sopa*.

flour
FLAU-uhr
harina

wheat
wit
trigo

hot dog
hat dag
perro caliente

DATO CURIOSO:
¡Cuidado! No confundas **flour** (*harina*) con **flower** (*flor*), aunque se pronuncien igual.

Food (Comida)

fud

DATO CURIOSO:
Los hablantes de inglés británico dicen **chips** para referirse a *papas fritas* en lugar de **fries**, que se usa en Estados Unidos.

fries

frayz

papas fritas

hamburger

HAHM-buhr-guhr

hamburguesa

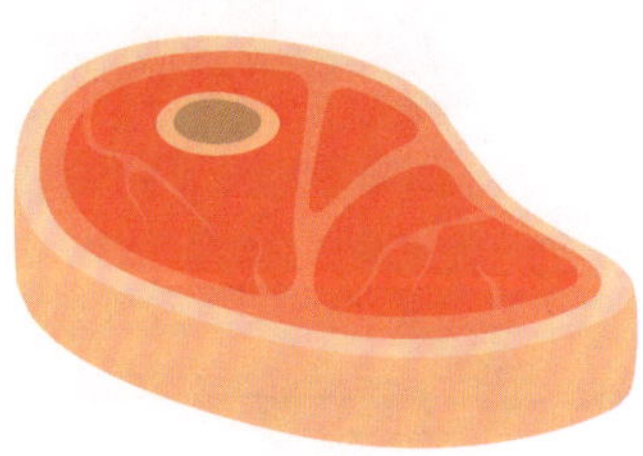

meat

mit

carne

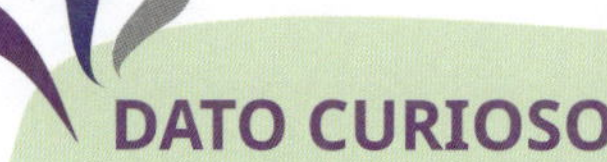

DATO CURIOSO:
Aunque la palabra **hamburger** incluye la palabra **ham** (*jamón*), una hamburguesa está hecha de carne de res. Además, hay muchos otros tipos de hamburguesas, como las **turkey burgers** (*hamburguesas de pavo*), las **tofu burgers** (*hamburguesas de tofu*) y las **veggie burgers** (*hamburguesas vegetarianas*).

ham

hahm

jamón

tuna

TU-nuh

atún

salmon

SAHM-uhn

salmón

salt
salt
sal

pepper
PEH-puhr
pimienta

DATO CURIOSO:
La palabra **pepper** se puede usar para referirse tanto a la especia (*pimienta*) como al vegetal (*pimiento* o *pimentón*).

ketchup
KEHCH-uhp
catsup

mustard
MUHS-tuhrd
mostaza

herbs
uhrbz
hierbas aromáticas

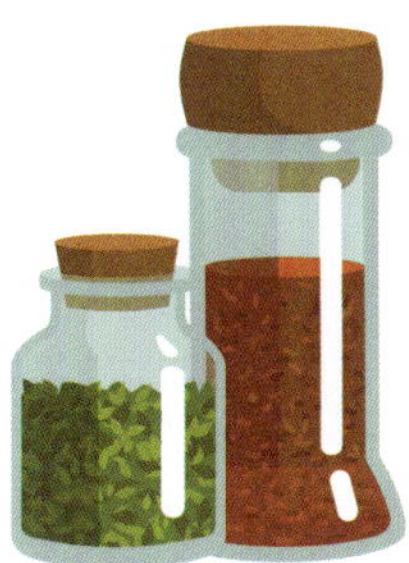

spices
SPAY-sihz
especias

oil
oyl
aceite

vinegar
VIH-nuh-guhr
vinagre

Food (Comida)
fud

sugar
SHOO-guhr
azúcar

chocolate
CHAK-liht
chocolate

ice cream
ays krim
helado

whipped cream
wihpt krim
crema batida

cake
keyk
pastel

DATO CURIOSO:
Si algo es **a piece of cake** (literalmente, *un pedazo de pastel*) o **easy as pie** (literalmente, *fácil como el pay*), quiere decir que es muy fácil de hacer. Una expresión similar en español sería *ser pan comido*.

pie
pay
pay

cookie
KOO-ki
galleta

candy
KAHN-di
dulce

Drinks (Bebidas)

drihngks

milk
mihlk
leche

tea
ti
té

coffee
KA-fi
café

water
WA-duhr
agua

sparkling water
SPARK-lihng WA-duhr
agua mineral

juice
jus
jugo

soda
SO-duh
refresco

DATO CURIOSO:
Hay otros nombres para **soda** en los EE. UU., como **pop**, **soda pop** y **soft drinks** (literalmente, *bebidas suaves*).

hot chocolate
hat CHAK-liht
chocolate caliente

Transportation (Medios de transporte)
trahns-puhr-TEY-shihn

car
kar
carro

taxi
TAHK-si
taxi

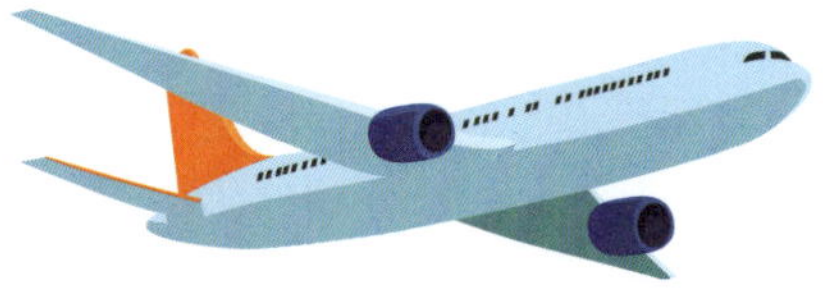

plane
pleyn
avión

truck
truhk
camión

van
vahn
camioneta

train
treyn
tren

subway
SUHB-wey
metro

DATO CURIOSO:
El metro se llama **the subway** en los Estados Unidos y **the tube** o **the underground** en Reino Unido. Algunos hablantes de inglés usan también el término **metro**.

motorcycle
MO-duhr-say-kuhl
motocicleta

bicycle
BAY-sih-kuhl
bicicleta

scooter
SKU-duhr
patinete

bus
buhs
autobús

garbage truck
GAR-bihj truhk
camión de basura

helicopter
HEH-lih-kap-tuhr
helicóptero

fire engine
FAY-uhr EHN-jihn
camión de bomberos

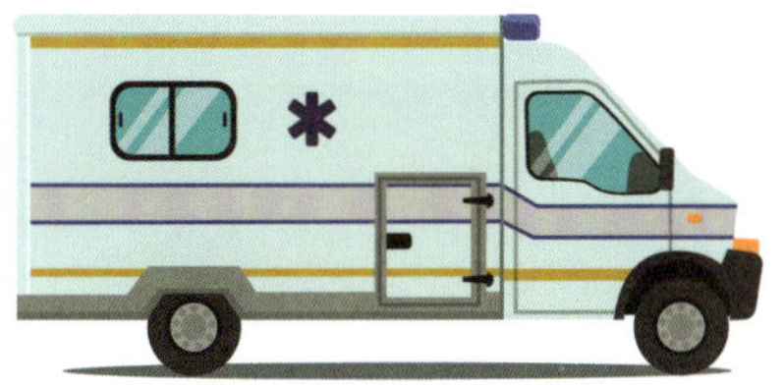

ambulance
AHM-byuh-lihns
ambulancia

Transportation
(Medios de transporte)
trahns-puhr-TEY-shihn

police car
puh-LIS kar
patrulla

digger
DIH-guhr
excavadora

DATO CURIOSO:
Se puede usar tanto la palabra **digger** como **excavator** para referirse a una *excavadora*.

ferry
FEHR-i
ferry

DATO CURIOSO:
La expresión **that ship has sailed** (literalmente, *ese barco ya zarpó*) sirve para referirse a una oportunidad perdida, como en español cuando se dice *ese tren ya pasó* o *ese pajarito ya voló*.

ship
shihp
barco

boat
bot
bote

sailboat
SEYL-bot
velero

hot-air balloon
had-EHR buh-LUN
globo aerostático

Clothing and accessories
(Ropa y accesorios)
KLO-thihng ahnd ahk-SEHS-uhr-iz

shirt
shuhrt
camisa

blouse
blaus
blusa

T-shirt
TI-shuhrt
playera

sweater
SWEH-duhr
suéter

vest
vehst
chaleco

pants
pahnts
pantalones

dress
drehs
vestido

socks
saks
calcetines

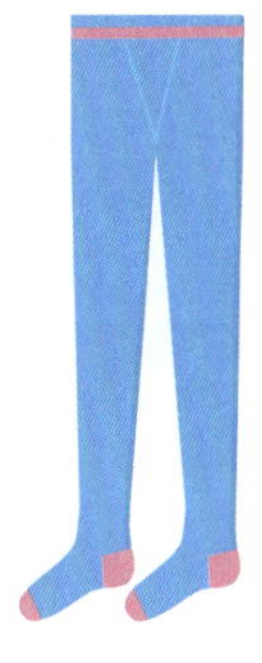

tights
tayts
medias

Clothing and accessories
(Ropa y accesorios)
KLO-thihng ahnd ahk-SEHS-uhr-iz

skirt
skuhrt
falda

coat
kot
abrigo

raincoat
REYN-kot
impermeable

umbrella
uhm-BREH-luh
paraguas

jacket
JAH-kiht
chamarra

scarf
skarf
bufanda

gloves
gluhvz
guantes

DATO CURIOSO:
To fit like a glove es una expresión que significa 'quedarle algo a alguien perfectamente'. En español se puede usar la misma expresión, *quedar como un guante*, o la expresión *venir como anillo al dedo*.

hat
haht
sombrero

baseball cap
BEYS-bal kahp
gorra

earrings
IR-ihngz
aretes

bracelet
BREYS-liht
pulsera

ring
rihng
anillo

necklace
NEHK-luhs
collar

belt
behlt
cinturón

shorts
shorts
short

glasses
GLAH-sihz
lentes

¡Escanea este código QR para escuchar las palabras!

Clothing and accessories
(Ropa y accesorios)
KLO-thihng ahnd ahk-SEHS-uhr-iz

underwear
UHN-duhr-wehr
ropa interior

bathing suit
BEY-thihng sut
traje de baño

sunglasses
SUHN-glah-sihz
lentes de sol

jeans
jinz
jeans

pajamas
puh-JA-muhz
piyama

DATO CURIOSO:
La palabra **pajamas** a veces se abrevia a **PJs**, que se pronuncia *PI-jeyz*.

tie
tay
corbata

bow tie
bo tay
moño

suit
sut
traje

Shoes (Calzado)

shuz

sneakers

SNI-kurz

tenis

DATO CURIOSO:
A veces a los **sneakers** se les llama **tennis shoes** (de ahí el préstamo *los tenis* en español). También se les llama **trainers** en el Reino Unido.

sandals

SAHN-duhlz

sandalias

DATO CURIOSO:
La palabra **flip-flop** imita el sonido que hace la gente al caminar con este tipo de sandalia.

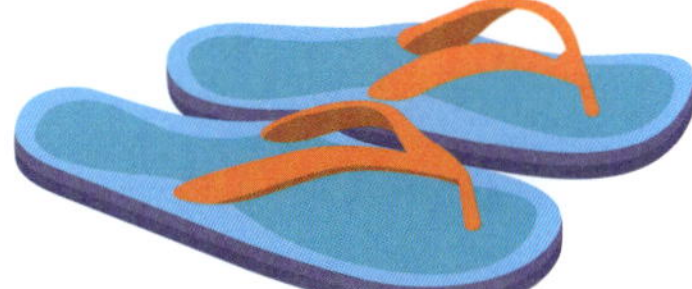

flip-flops

FLIHP-flaps

chanclas

boots

buts

botas

high heels

hay hilz

tacones

slippers

SLIH-puhrz

pantuflas

rain boots

reyn buts

botas de lluvia

The body (El cuerpo)
thuh BA-di

head
hehd
cabeza

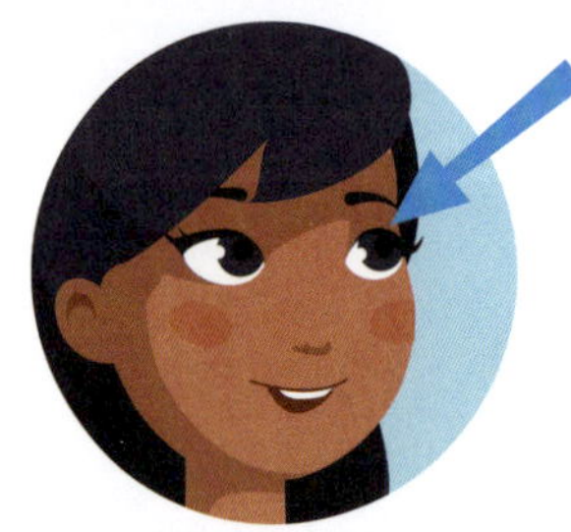

eye
ay
ojo

ear
ir
oreja

eyebrow
AY-brau
ceja

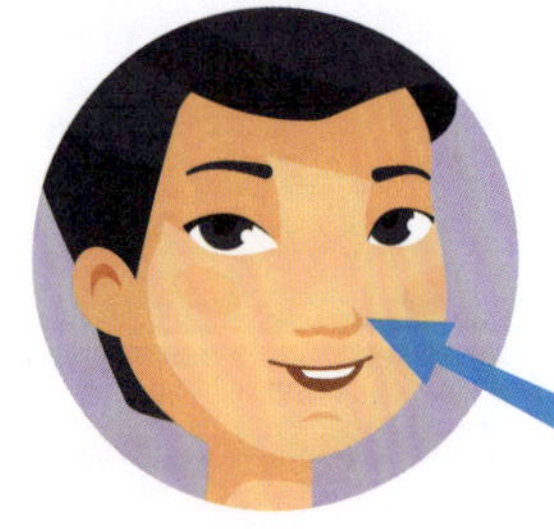

nose
noz
nariz

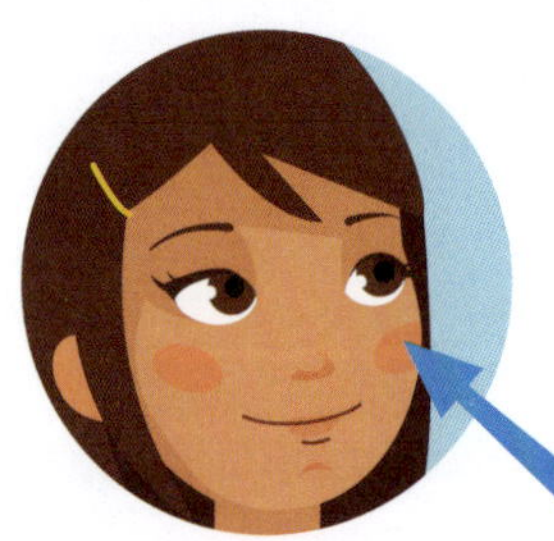

cheek
chik
mejilla

chin
chihn
barbilla

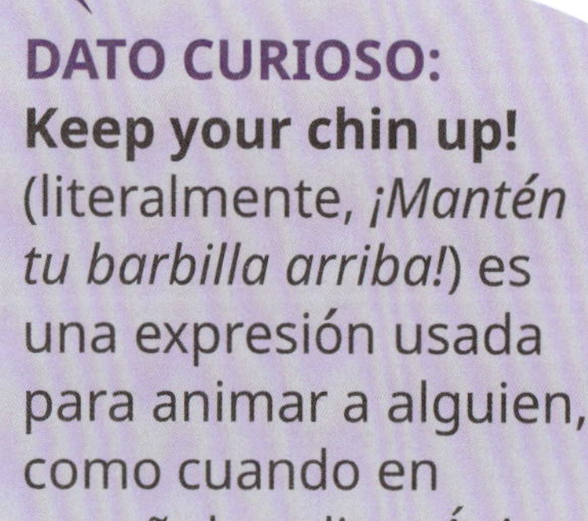

DATO CURIOSO:
Keep your chin up!
(literalmente, *¡Mantén tu barbilla arriba!*) es una expresión usada para animar a alguien, como cuando en español se dice *¡Ánimo!*

mouth
mauth
boca

lips
lihps
labios

teeth
tith
dientes

face
feys
cara

hair
hehr
cabello

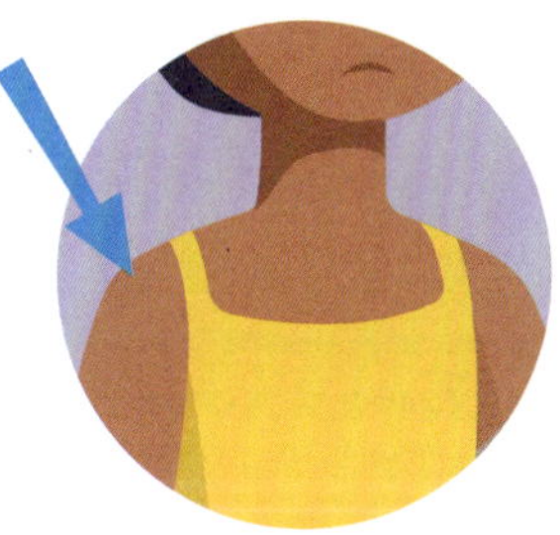

shoulder
SHOL-duhr
hombro

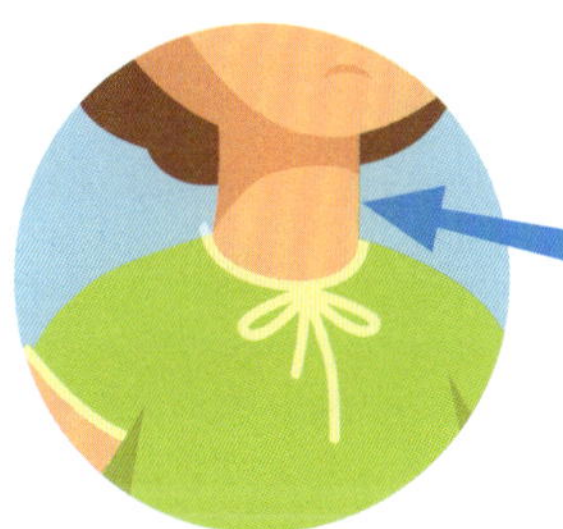

neck
nehk
cuello

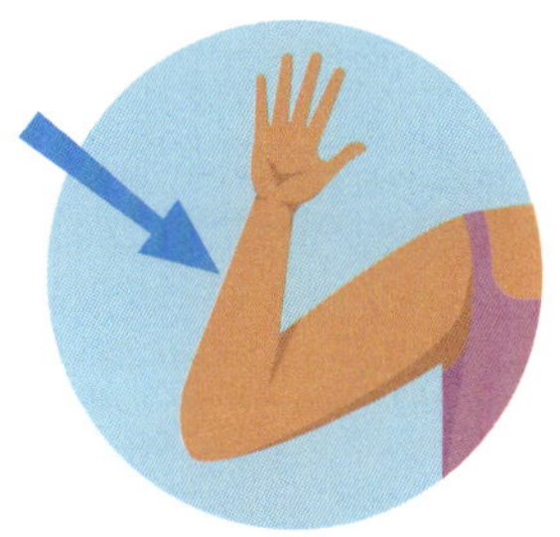

arm
arm
brazo

DATO CURIOSO:
Al igual que en español, si le das la bienvenida a alguien **with open arms** (*con los brazos abiertos*), le das la bienvenida de manera muy amable.

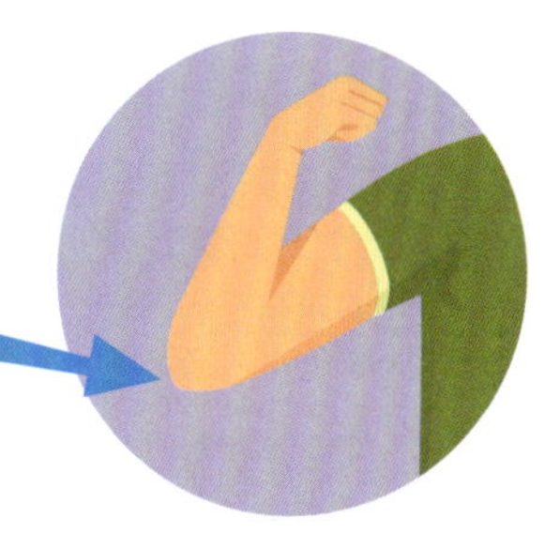

elbow
EHL-bo
codo

The body (El cuerpo)
thuh BA-di

hand
hahnd
mano

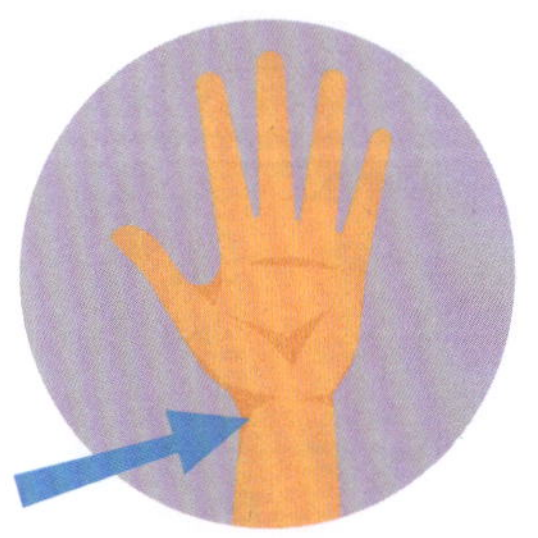

wrist
rihst
muñeca

finger
FIHNG-guhr
dedo

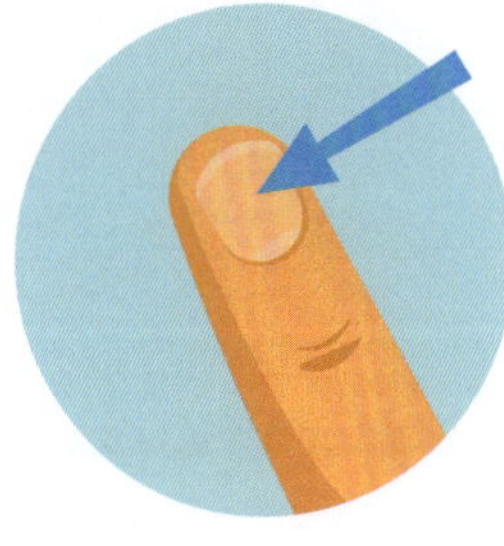

fingernail
FIHNG-guhr-neyl
uña

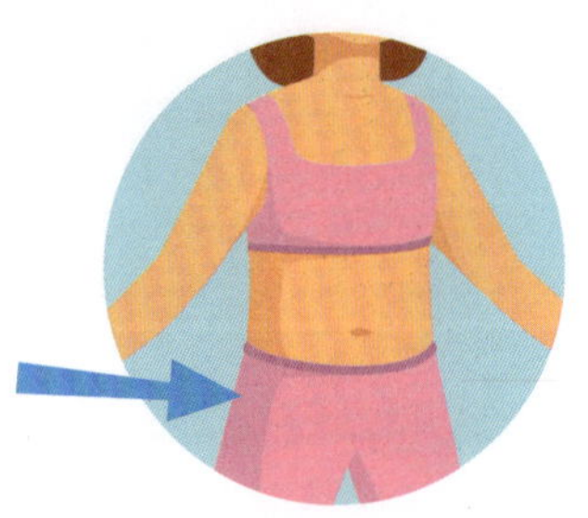

hip
hihp
cadera

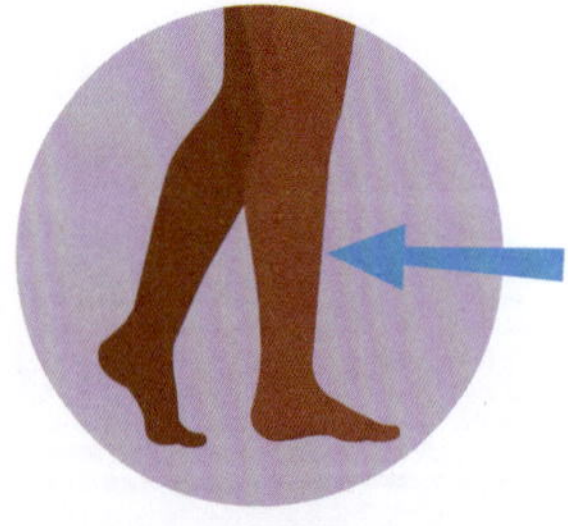

leg
lehg
pierna

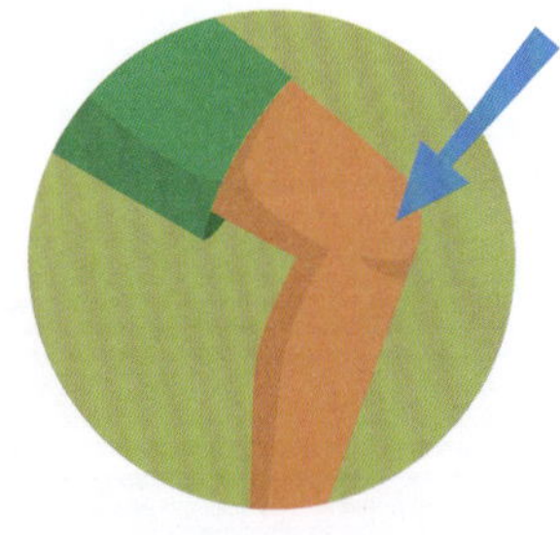

knee
ni
rodilla

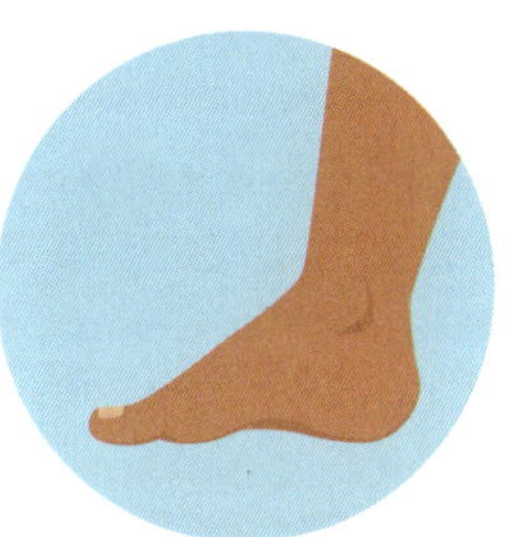

foot
foot
pie

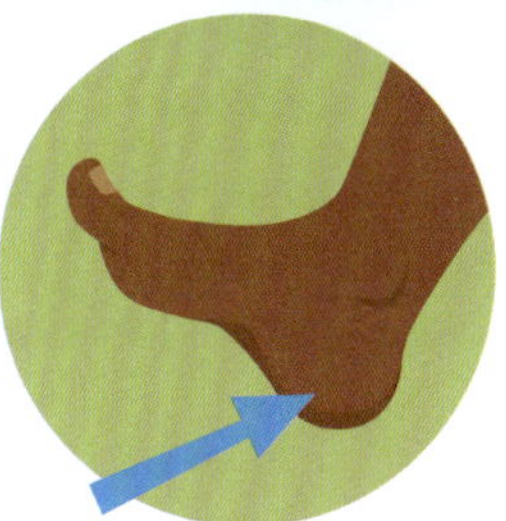

heel
hil
talón

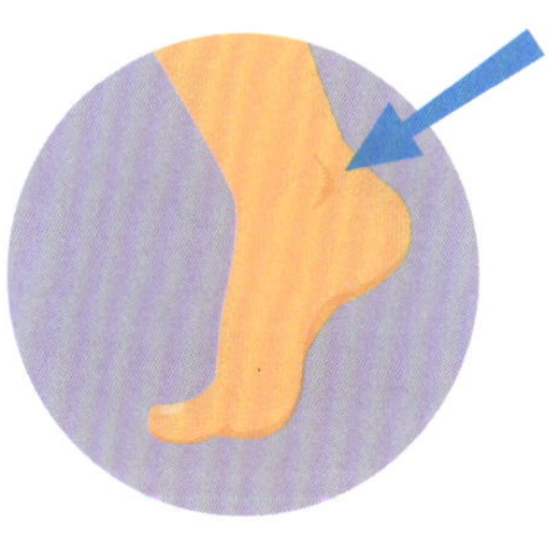

ankle
AHNG-kuhl
tobillo

toe
to
dedo del pie

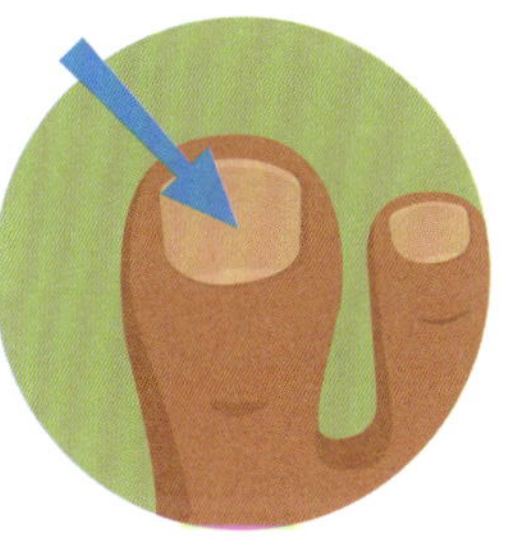

toenail
TO-neyl
uña del pie

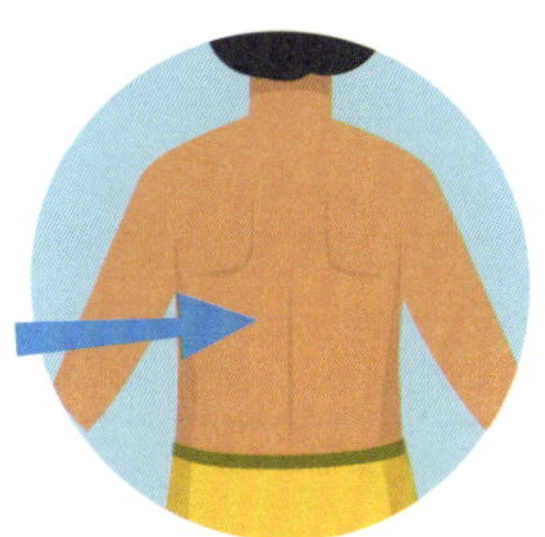

back
bahk
espalda

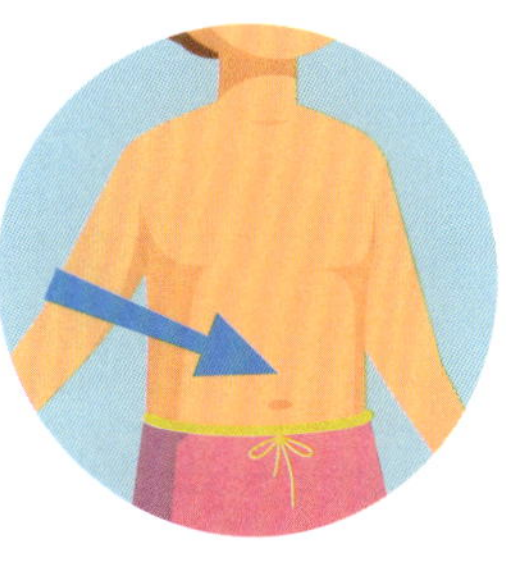

tummy
TUH-mi
barriga

Family (Familia)

FAHM-li

mom
mam
mamá

dad
dahd
papá

parents
PEHR-ihnts
papás

daughter
DA-duhr
hija

son
suhn
hijo

sister
SIHS-tuhr
hermana

brother
BRUH-thuhr
hermano

grandmother
GRAHND-muh-thuhr
abuela

grandfather
GRAHND-fa-thuhr
abuelo

uncle
UHNG-kuhl
tío

aunt
ahnt
tía

baby
BEY-bi
bebé

cousin
KUH-zihn
primo

DATO CURIOSO:
Mientras en español se usa *el primo* y *la prima* para distinguir entre los primos de diferente sexo, en inglés se usa **cousin** para ambos.

nephew
NEH-fyu
sobrino

niece
nis
sobrina

grandson
GRAHND-suhn
nieto

granddaughter
GRAHN-da-duhr
nieta

At home (En la casa)
aht hom

apartment
uh-PART-mihnt
apartamento

stairs
stehrz
escaleras

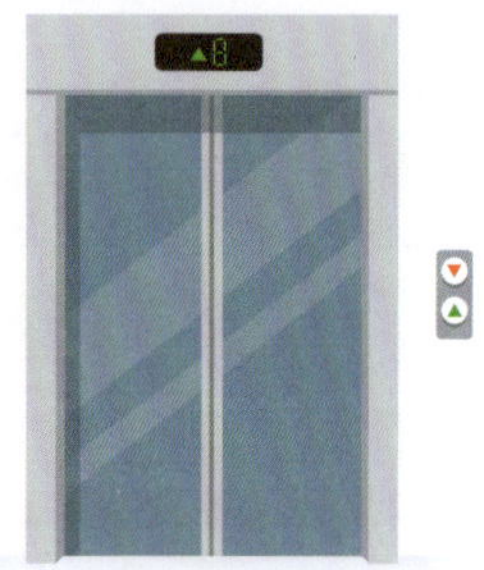

elevator
EH-luh-vey-duhr
elevador

roof
ruf
techo

balcony
BAHL-kuh-ni
balcón

hallway
HAL-wey
pasillo

window
WIHN-do
ventana

door
dor
puerta

room
rum
cuarto

rug
ruhg
alfombra

floor
flor
piso

couch
kauch
sofá

DATO CURIOSO:
Un **couch** también se puede llamar **sofa**, como *sofá* en español.

shelf
shehlf
estante

chair
chehr
silla

table
TEY-buhl
mesa

coffee table
KA-fi TEY-buhl
mesa de centro

At home (En la casa)
aht hom

television
TEH-luh-vih-zhihn
televisión

DATO CURIOSO:
La palabra **television** normalmente se acorta a **TV**. En inglés británico coloquial también se usa el término **telly**.

bed
behd
cama

pillow
PIH-lo
almohada

clock
klak
reloj

DATO CURIOSO:
En inglés se usa la palabra **wristwatch** (o simplemente **watch**) para referirse al reloj que llevas puesto en la muñeca.

painting
PEYN-tihng
cuadro

DATO CURIOSO:
La palabra **painting** puede usarse como sustantivo (*cuadro*) o para formar un verbo en tiempo continuo, p. ej. **I'm painting** (*estoy pintando*).

dresser
DREH-suhr
cómoda

DATO CURIOSO: Un **fan** también puede referirse a un admirador entusiasta, igual que en español.

fan
fahn
ventilador

computer
kuhm-PYU-duhr
computadora

cell phone
SEHL-fon
celular

lamp
lahmp
lámpara

bookcase
BOOK-keys
librero

desk
dehsk
escritorio

¡Escanea este código QR para escuchar las palabras!

At home (En la casa)
aht hom

vase
veyz
florero

curtain
KUHR-tihn
cortina

cushion
KOO-shihn
cojín

toys
toyz
juguetes

garden
GAR-dihn
jardín

attic
AH-dihk
ático

basement
BEYS-mihnt
sótano

washer
WA-shuhr
lavadora

dryer
DRAY-uhr
secadora

In the kitchen (En la cocina)

ihn thuh KIH-chihn

refrigerator
rih-FRIHJ-uhr-ey-duhr
refrigerador

DATO CURIOSO:
Refrigerator normalmente se acorta a **fridge** en inglés, igual que *refrigerador* se acorta a *refri*.

stove
stov
estufa

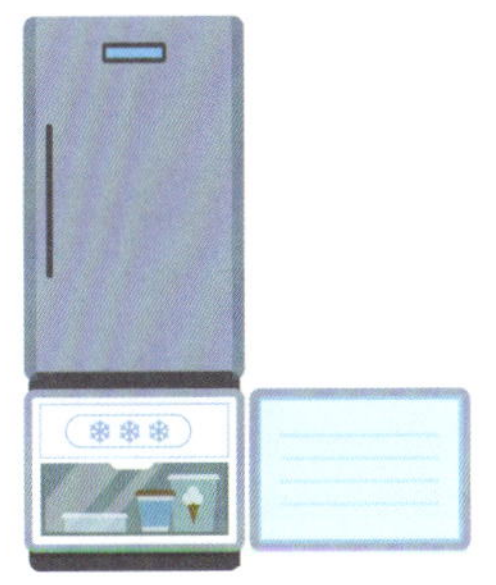

freezer
FRI-zuhr
congelador

pan
pahn
sartén

pot
pat
olla

DATO CURIOSO:
Otro nombre para el **garbage can** es **trash can**. En el Reino Unido también se le llama **rubbish bin**.

garbage can
GAR-bihj kahn
bote de basura

dishwasher
DIHSH-wa-shuhr
lavaplatos

In the kitchen (En la cocina)
ihn thuh KIH-chihn

microwave
MAY-kro-weyv
microondas

toaster
TOS-duhr
tostador

apron
EY-prihn
delantal

oven
UH-vihn
horno

DATO CURIOSO:
Sink también es un verbo que significa 'hundir'.

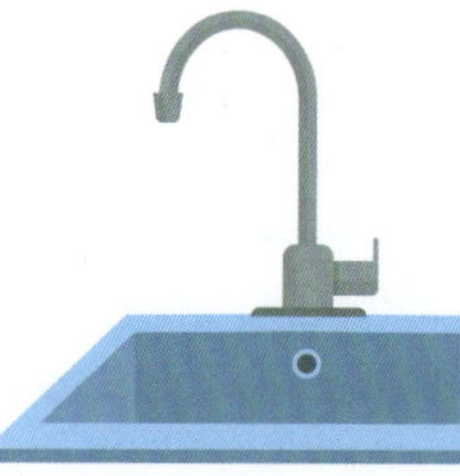

kitchen sink
KIH-chihn sihngk
fregadero

faucet
FA-siht
llave

blender
BLEHN-duhr
licuadora

tea kettle
ti KEH-duhl
tetera

At the table (En la mesa)

aht thuh TEY-buhl

fork
fork
tenedor

knife
nayf
cuchillo

spoon
spun
cuchara

glass
glahs
vaso

plate
pleyt
plato

DATO CURIOSO:
I have a lot on my plate (literalmente, *tengo mucho en mi plato*) es una expresión que significa 'tengo muchas cosas entre manos'.

bowl
bol
bol

cup
kuhp
taza

napkin
NAHP-kihn
servilleta

At the table (En la mesa)
aht thuh TEY-buhl

pitcher
PIH-chuhr
jarra

menu
MEH-nyu
menú

tablecloth
TEY-buhl-klath
mantel

breakfast
BREHK-fihst
desayuno

lunch
luhnch
almuerzo

dinner
DIH-nuhr
cena

dessert
dih-ZUHRT
postre

DATO CURIOSO: Ten cuidado de no confundir **dessert** (*postre*) con **desert** (*desierto*).

dishes
DIH-shihz
vajilla

Bathtime (Hora del baño)

BAHTH-taym

toothbrush
TUTH-bruhsh
cepillo de dientes

toothpaste
TUTH-peyst
pasta de dientes

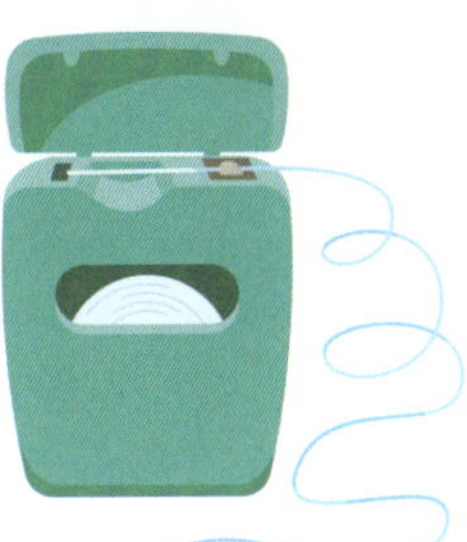

floss
flas
hilo dental

sink
sihngk
lavabo

hairbrush
HEHR-bruhsh
cepillo

DATO CURIOSO: Hairbrush normalmente se acorta a **brush**.

comb
kom
peine

toilet paper
TOY-liht PEY-puhr
papel higiénico

toilet
TOY-liht
inodoro

Bathtime (Hora del baño)
BAHTH-taym

bathtub
BAHTH-tuhb
bañera

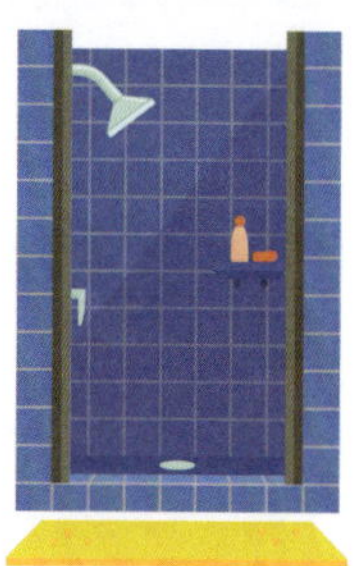

shower
SHAU-uhr
ducha

DATO CURIOSO:
Una **shower** también se refiere a una fiesta para celebrar algo, como una **bridal shower** (*bridal shower* o *shower para la novia*) o una **baby shower** (*baby shower* o *fiesta del bebé*).

towel
TAU-uhl
toalla

soap
sop
jabón

shampoo
shahm-PU
champú

lotion
LO-shihn
crema

mirror
MIR-uhr
espejo

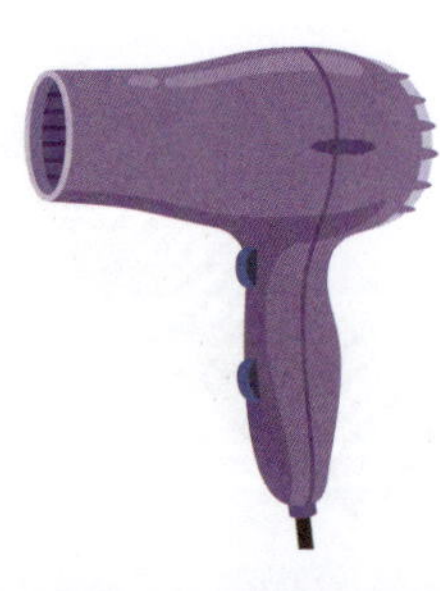

hair dryer
HEHR-dray-uhr
secadora de cabello

At school (En la escuela)
aht skul

pencil
PEHN-suhl
lápiz

scissors
SIH-zuhrz
tijeras

ruler
RU-luhr
regla

eraser
uh-REY-suhr
goma

book
book
libro

blackboard
BLAHK-bord
pizarrón

whiteboard
WAYT-bord
pizarrón blanco

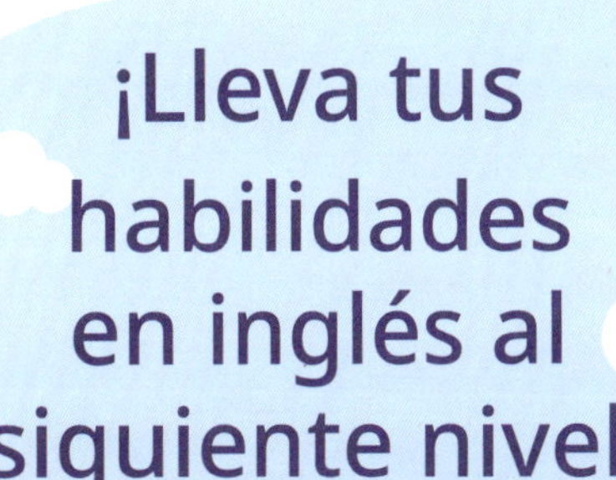

Regístrate en RosettaStone.com.

At school (En la escuela)
aht skul

uniform
YU-nih-form
uniforme

cafeteria
kah-fih-TI-ri-uh
comedor

lunchbox
LUHNCH-baks
lonchera

notebook
NOT-book
cuaderno

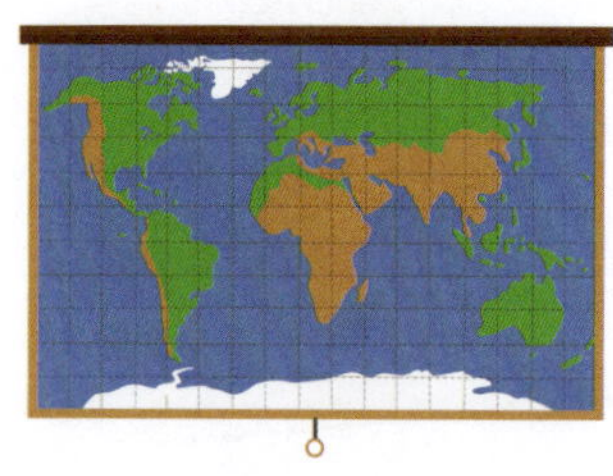

map
mahp
mapa

crayon
KREY-an
crayón

marker
MAR-kuhr
marcador

pen
pehn
bolígrafo

DATO CURIOSO:
Pen pals son personas que se escriben con regularidad, especialmente por carta.

Sports (Deportes)
sports

soccer
SA-kuhr
futbol

football
FOOT-bal
futbol americano

DATO CURIOSO:
En algunos países de habla inglesa, *futbol* se dice **football** en lugar de **soccer**.

basketball
BAHS-kiht-bal
basquetbol

tennis
TEH-nihs
tenis

cycling
SAY-klihng
ciclismo

skiing
SKI-ihng
esquí

ice-skating
ays SKEY-dihng
patinaje sobre hielo

golf
galf
golf

Sports (Deportes)

sports

swimming
SWIHM-ihng

natación

diving
DAY-vihng

salto

rowing
RO-ihng

remo

baseball
BEYS-bal

beisbol

hiking
HAY-kihng

senderismo

running
RUHN-ihng

correr

dancing
DAHNS-ihng

baile

horseback riding
HORS-bahk RAY-dihng

equitación

sailing
SEYL-ihng

vela

surfing
SUHR-fihng
surf

skateboarding
SKEYT-bor-dihng
patinaje en tabla

ice hockey
ays HA-ki
hockey sobre hielo

volleyball
VA-li-bal
voleibol

wrestling
REHS-lihng
lucha

martial arts
MAR-shuhl arts
artes marciales

table tennis
TEY-buhl TEHN-ihs
tenis de mesa

DATO CURIOSO:
Table tennis a veces también se llama **ping-pong**, como en español.

gymnastics
jihm-NAHS-tihks
gimnasia

Sports equipment
(Artículos deportivos)
sports uh-KWIHP-mihnt

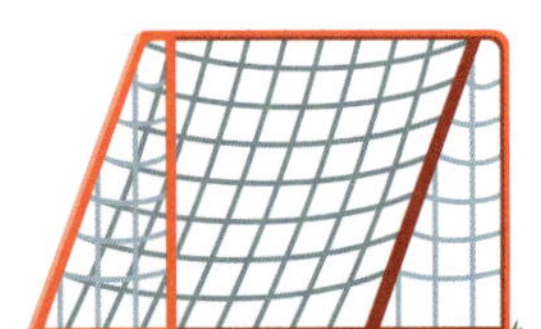

goal
gol
portería

basketball hoop
BAHS-kiht-bal hup
aro de basquetbol

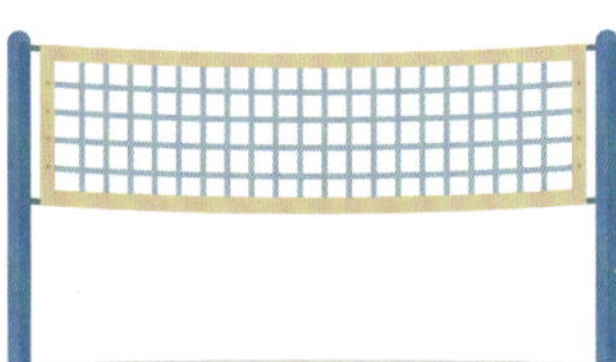

net
neht
red

baseball bat
BEYS-bal baht
bate de beisbol

DATO CURIOSO:
Si **the ball's in your court** (literalmente, *la pelota está en tu cancha*), te toca a ti pasar a la acción o tomar la próxima decisión.

ball
bal
pelota

ice skates
ays skeyts
patines de hielo

helmet
HEHL-miht
casco

tennis racket
TEHN-ihs RAH-kiht
raqueta de tenis

Frases útiles
(Useful phrases)

¡Hola!
Hello!
heh-LO

Buenos días.
Good morning.
good MOR-nihng

Buenas tardes.
Good afternoon.
good ahf-duhr-NUN

Buenas noches.
Good night.
good nayt

Hola, me llamo...
Hi, my name is...
hay may neym ihz

Mucho gusto.
Pleased to meet you.
plizd tu mit yu

Bienvenido(s)/ Bienvenida(s).
Welcome.
WEHL-kuhm

Adiós.
Goodbye.
good-BAY

¡Hasta luego!
See you later!
si yu LEY-duhr

¿Qué tal?
What's up?
wuhts uhp

¿Cómo estás?
How are you?
hau ar yu

Estoy bien, ¿y tú?
I'm well, and you?
aym wehl ahnd yu

Muchas gracias.
Thank you very much.
thahngk yu VEH-ri muhch

De nada.
You're welcome.
yuhr WEHL-kuhm

What's up? es una manera menos formal de preguntar **How are you?** La respuesta suele ser **Not much.**

No entiendo.
I don't understand.
ay dont uhn-duhr-STAHND

Las palabras en inglés no siempre cambian dependiendo de quien hable o de con quien estés hablando. Por ejemplo, se usa **welcome** sin importar si le estás dando la bienvenida a una mujer o a un hombre, o a una o a varias personas.

Frases útiles
(Useful phrases)

¿Dónde está el baño?
Where is the bathroom?
wehr ihz thuh BAHTH-rum

¿Hablas español?
Do you speak Spanish?
du yu spik SPAH-nihsh

En inglés se usa la palabra **you** para *tú*, *vos*, *usted*, *ustedes*, *vosotros* y *vosotras*.

¿Cuántos años tienes?
How old are you?
hau old ar yu

Tengo __ años.
I'm __ years old.
aym __ yirz old

¿Me podrías ayudar?
Could you help me?
kood yu hehlp mi

¿Nos podrías tomar una foto?
Could you take our picture?
kood yu teyk aur PIHK-chuhr

Por favor
Please
pliz

Sí   **No**
Yes   No
yehs   *no*

La palabra **okay** a veces se escribe **OK**.

De acuerdo.
Okay.
o-KEY

Lo siento.
I'm sorry.
aym SAW-ri

¿Cuánto cuesta esto?
How much does this cost?
hau muhch duhz thihs kast

¡Buen provecho!
Enjoy your meal!
ehn-JOY yuhr mil

Con permiso.
Excuse me.
ehk-SKYUZ mi

¡Aquí!
Here!
hir

Lista de vocabulario

A

abeja
bee
bi

abrigo
coat
kot

abuela
grandmother
GRAHND-muh-thuhr

abuelo
grandfather
GRAHND-fa-thuhr

aceite
oil
oyl

aceituna
olive
A-lihv

agua
water
WA-duhr

agua mineral
sparkling water
SPARK-lihng WA-duhr

aguacate
avocado
a-vuh-KA-do

ajo
garlic
GAR-lihk

alcachofa
artichoke
AR-dih-chok

alfombra
rug
ruhg

almendra
almond
AL-mihnd

almohada
pillow
PIH-lo

almuerzo
lunch
luhnch

amarillo
yellow
YEH-lo

ambulancia
ambulance
AHM-byuh-lihns

anaranjado
orange
OR-ihnj

anillo
ring
rihng

apartamento
apartment
uh-PART-mihnt

apio
celery
SEH-luh-ri

araña
spider
SPAY-duhr

arándano azul
blueberry
BLU-beh-ri

arándano rojo
cranberry
KRAHN-behr-i

ardilla
squirrel
skwuhrl

aretes
earrings
IR-ihngz

aro de basquetbol
basketball hoop
BAHS-kiht-bal hup

arroz
rice
rays

artes marciales
martial arts
MAR-shuhl arts

ático
attic
AH-dihk

atún
tuna
TU-nuh

autobús
bus
buhs

avellana
hazelnut
HEY-zuhl-nuht

avena
oatmeal
OT-mil

avión
plane
pleyn

azúcar
sugar
SHOO-guhr

azul
blue
blu

azul claro
light blue
layt blu

azul oscuro
dark blue
dark blu

B

baile
dancing
DAHNS-ihng

balcón
balcony
BAHL-kuh-ni

ballena
whale
weyl

bañera
bathtub
BAHTH-tuhb

barbilla
chin
chihn

barco
ship
shihp

barriga
tummy
TUH-mi

basquetbol
basketball
BAHS-kiht-bal

bate de beisbol
baseball bat
BEYS-bal baht

bebé
baby
BEY-bi

beisbol
baseball
BEYS-bal

berenjena
eggplant
EHG-plahnt

bicicleta
bicycle
BAY-sih-kuhl

blanco
white
wayt

blusa
blouse
blaus

boca
mouth
mauth

bol
bowl
bol

bolígrafo
pen
pehn

botas
boots
buts

botas de lluvia
rain boots
reyn buts

bote
boat
bot

bote de basura
garbage can
GAR-bihj kahn

brazo
arm
arm

brócoli
broccoli
BRA-kuh-li

bufanda
scarf
skarf

búho
owl
aul

C

caballito de mar
seahorse
SI-hors

caballo
horse
hors

cabello
hair
hehr

cabeza
head
hehd

cabra
goat
got

cacahuate
peanut
PI-nuht

cadera
hip
hihp

café (color)
brown
braun

café (bebida)
coffee
KA-fi

calabacita
zucchini
zu-KI-ni

calabaza
pumpkin
PUHMP-kihn

calcetines
socks
saks

cama
bed
behd

camello
camel
KAH-muhl

camión
truck
truhk

camión de basura
garbage truck
GAR-bihj truhk

camión de bomberos
fire engine
FAY-uhr EHN-jihn

camioneta
van
vahn

camisa
shirt
shuhrt

camote
sweet potato
swit puh-TEY-do

cangrejo
crab
krahb

canguro
kangaroo
kahng-guh-RU

caqui
persimmon
puhr-SIH-mihn

cara
face
feys

carne
meat
mit

carro
car
kar

casco
helmet
HEHL-miht

castaña
chestnut
CHEHS-nuht

catorce
fourteen
for-TIN

catsup
ketchup
KEHCH-uhp

cebolla
onion
UHN-yihn

cebra
zebra
ZI-bruh

ceja
eyebrow
AY-brau

celular
cell phone
SEHL-fon

cena
dinner
DIH-nuhr

cepillo
hairbrush
HEHR-bruhsh

cepillo de dientes
toothbrush
TUTH-bruhsh

cerdo
pig
pihg

cereales
cereal
SIR-i-uhl

cereza
cherry
CHEH-ri

cero
zero
ZI-ro

chabacano
apricot
AH-prih-kat

chaleco
vest
vehst

chalote
shallot
SHAH-liht

chamarra
jacket
JAH-kiht

champiñón
mushroom
MUHSH-rum

champú
shampoo
shahm-PU

chanclas
flip-flops
FLIHP-flaps

chícharos
peas
piz

chocolate
chocolate
CHAK-liht

chocolate caliente
hot chocolate
hat CHAK-liht

ciclismo
cycling
SAY-klihng

ciempiés
centipede
SEHN-tih-pid

cien
one hundred
wuhn HUHN-drihd

cinco
five
fayv

cincuenta
fifty
FIHF-di

cinturón
belt
behlt

círculo
circle
SUHR-kuhl

ciruela
plum
pluhm

ciruela pasa
prune
prun

coco
coconut
KO-kuh-nuht

Lista de vocabulario

cocodrilo
crocodile
KRA-kuh-dayl

codo
elbow
EHL-bo

cojín
cushion
KOO-shihn

col
cabbage
KAH-bihj

coles de Bruselas
Brussels sprouts
BRUH-suhl sprauts

col rizada
kale
keyl

coliflor
cauliflower
KA-luh-flau-uhr

collar
necklace
NEHK-luhs

comedor
cafeteria
kah-fih-TI-ri-uh

cómoda
dresser
DREH-suhr

computadora
computer
kuhm-PYU-duhr

conejo
rabbit
RAH-biht

congelador
freezer
FRI-zuhr

corazón
heart
hart

corbata
tie
tay

correr
running
RUHN-ihng

cortina
curtain
KUHR-tihn

crayón
crayon
KREY-an

crema
lotion
LO-shihn

crema batida
whipped cream
wihpt krim

cuaderno
notebook
NOT-book

cuadrado
square
skwehr

cuadro
painting
PEYN-tihng

cuarenta
forty
FOR-di

cuarto
room
rum

cuatro
four
for

cuchara
spoon
spun

cuchillo
knife
nayf

cuello
neck
nehk

D

dátil
date
deyt

dedo
finger
FIHNG-guhr

dedo del pie
toe
to

delantal
apron
EY-prihn

delfín
dolphin
DAL-fihn

desayuno
breakfast
BREHK-fihst

diecinueve
nineteen
nayn-TIN

dieciocho
eighteen
ey-TIN

dieciséis
sixteen
sihks-TIN

diecisiete
seventeen
seh-vuhn-TIN

dientes
teeth
tith

diez
ten
tehn

doce
twelve
twehlv

dos
two
tu

ducha
shower
SHAU-uhr

dulce
candy
KAHN-di

durazno
peach
pich

E

ejotes
green beans
grin binz

elefante
elephant
EH-lih-fihnt

elevador
elevator
EH-luh-vey-duhr

ensalada
salad
SAH-luhd

equitación
horseback riding
HORS-bahk RAY-dihng

erizo
hedgehog
HEHJ-hag

escaleras
stairs
stehrz

escarabajo
beetle
BI-duhl

escritorio
desk
dehsk

espalda
back
bahk

espárrago
asparagus
uh-SPEH-rih-gihs

especias
spices
SPAY-sihz

espejo
mirror
MIR-uhr

espinacas
spinach
SPIH-nihch

esquí
skiing
SKI-ihng

estante
shelf
shehlf

estrella
star
star

estrella de mar
sea star
si star

estufa
stove
stov

excavadora
digger
DIH-guhr

F

falda
skirt
skuhrt

ferry
ferry
FEHR-i

fideos
noodles
NU-duhlz

flamenco
flamingo
fluh-MIHNG-go

florero
vase
veyz

foca
seal
sil

frambuesa
raspberry
RAHZ-beh-ri

fregadero
kitchen sink
KIH-chihn sihngk

fresa
strawberry
STRA-beh-ri

frijoles
beans
binz

futbol
soccer
SA-kuhr

futbol americano
football
FOOT-bal

G

galleta
cookie
KOO-ki

gallina
hen
hehn

Lista de vocabulario

gallo
rooster
RU-stuhr

ganso
goose
gus

gato
cat
kaht

gimnasia
gymnastics
jihm-NAHS-tihks

globo aerostático
hot-air balloon
had-EHR buh-LUN

golf
golf
galf

goma
eraser
uh-REY-suhr

gorila
gorilla
guh-RIH-luh

gorra
baseball cap
BEYS-bal kahp

gris
gray
grey

guantes
gloves
gluhvz

guayaba
guava
GWA-vuh

gusano
worm
wuhrm

H

hamburguesa
hamburger
HAHM-buhr-guhr

hámster
hamster
HAHM-stuhr

harina
flour
FLAU-uhr

helado
ice cream
ays krim

helicóptero
helicopter
HEH-lih-kap-tuhr

hermana
sister
SIHS-tuhr

hermano
brother
BRUH-thuhr

hexágono
hexagon
HEHK-suh-gan

hierbas aromáticas
herbs
uhrbz

higo
fig
fihg

hija
daughter
DA-duhr

hijo
son
suhn

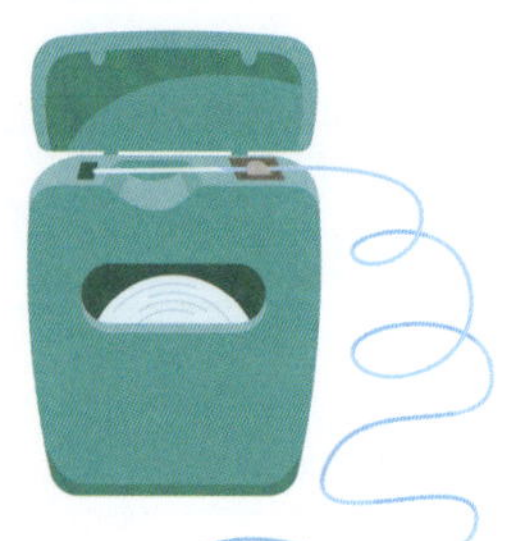

hilo dental
floss
flas

hipopótamo
hippopotamus
hih-po-PA-duh-mihs

hockey sobre hielo
ice hockey
ays HA-ki

hombro
shoulder
SHOL-duhr

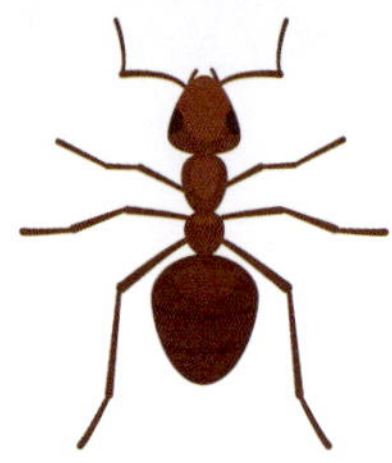

hormiga
ant
ahnt

horno
oven
UH-vihn

huevo
egg
ehg

I

impermeable
raincoat
REYN-kot

inodoro
toilet
TOY-liht

J

jabón
soap
sop

jamón
ham
hahm

jardín
garden
GAR-dihn

jarra	langosta		lucha

jarra
pitcher
PIH-chuhr

jeans
jeans
jinz

jengibre
ginger
JIHN-juhr

jirafa
giraffe
jih-RAHF

jugo
juice
jus

juguetes
toys
toyz

K

kiwi
kiwi
KI-wi

koala
koala
ko-A-luh

L

labios
lips
lihps

lámpara
lamp
lahmp

langosta
lobster
LAB-stuhr

lápiz
pencil
PEHN-suhl

lavabo
sink
sihngk

lavadora
washer
WA-shuhr

lavaplatos
dishwasher
DIHSH-wa-shuhr

leche
milk
mihlk

lechuga
lettuce
LEH-dihs

lentejas
lentils
LEHN-tuhls

lentes
glasses
GLAH-sihz

lentes de sol
sunglasses
SUHN-glah-sihz

león
lion
LAY-ihn

libélula
dragonfly
DRAH-gihn-flay

librero
bookcase
BOOK-keys

libro
book
book

licuadora
blender
BLEHN-duhr

lima
lemon
LEH-mihn

limón
lime
laym

llave
faucet
FA-siht

lobo
wolf
woolf

lonchera
lunchbox
LUHNCH-baks

loro
parrot
PEH-riht

lucha
wrestling
REHS-lihng

luciérnaga
firefly
FAY-uhr-flay

M

maíz
corn
korn

mamá
mom
mam

mango
mango
MAHNG-go

mano
hand
hahnd

mantel
tablecloth
TEY-buhl-klath

mantequilla
butter
BUH-duhr

manzana
apple
AH-puhl

mapa
map
mahp

Lista de vocabulario

mapache
raccoon
rah-KUN

maracuyá
passion fruit
PAH-shihn frut

marcador
marker
MAR-kuhr

mariposa
butterfly
BUH-duhr-flay

medias
tights
tayts

mejilla
cheek
chik

melón
melon
MEH-lihn

menú
menu
MEH-nyu

mermelada
jam
jahm

mesa
table
TEY-buhl

mesa de centro
coffee table
KA-fi TEY-buhl

metro
subway
SUHB-wey

microondas
microwave
MAY-kro-weyv

miel
honey
HUH-ni

mono
monkey
MUHNG-ki

moño
bow tie
bo tay

morado
purple
PUHR-puhl

mosca
fly
flay

mosquito
mosquito
muh-SKI-do

mostaza
mustard
MUHS-tuhrd

motocicleta
motorcycle
MO-duhr-say-kuhl

muñeca
wrist
rihst

murciélago
bat
baht

N

naranja
orange
OR-ihnj

nariz
nose
noz

natación
swimming
SWIHM-ihng

negro
black
blahk

nieta
granddaughter
GRAHN-da-duhr

nieto
grandson
GRAHND-suhn

noventa
ninety
NAYN-di

nueve
nine
nayn

nuez
walnut
WAL-nuht

nuez pecana
pecan
pih-KAN

nuez de la India
cashew
KAH-shu

O

ochenta
eighty
EY-di

ocho
eight
eyt

ojo
eye
ay

olla
pot
pat

once
eleven
uh-LEH-vihn

oreja
ear
ir

oruga
caterpillar
KAH-duhr-pih-luhr

oso
bear
behr

óvalo
oval
O-vuhl

oveja
sheep
ship

P

pájaro
bird
buhrd

pan
bread
brehd

panda
panda
PAHN-duh

pantalones
pants
pahnts

pantuflas
slippers
SLIH-puhrz

papa
potato
puh-TEY-do

papá
dad
dahd

papás
parents
PEHR-ihnts

papas fritas
fries
frayz

papaya
papaya
puh-PAY-yuh

papel higiénico
toilet paper
TOY-liht PEY-puhr

paraguas
umbrella
uhm-BREH-luh

pasas
raisins
REY-zihnz

pasillo
hallway
HAL-wey

pasta
pasta
PA-stuh

pasta de dientes
toothpaste
TUTH-peyst

pastel
cake
keyk

patinaje en tabla
skateboarding
SKEYT-bor-dihng

patinaje sobre hielo
ice-skating
ays SKEY-dihng

patines de hielo
ice skates
ays skeyts

patinete
scooter
SKU-duhr

pato
duck
duhk

patrulla
police car
puh-LIS kar

pavo
turkey
TUHR-ki

pay
pie
pay

peine
comb
kom

pelota
ball
bal

pepino
cucumber
KYU-kuhm-buhr

pera
pear
pehr

perro
dog
dag

perro caliente
hot dog
hat dag

pez
fish
fihsh

pie
foot
foot

pierna
leg
lehg

pimienta
pepper
PEH-puhr

pimiento
bell pepper
behl PEH-puhr

piña
pineapple
PAYN-ah-puhl

pingüino
penguin
PEYNG-gwihn

piso
floor
flor

Lista de vocabulario

pistacho
pistachio
pih-STAH-shi-o

piyama
pajamas
puh-JA-muhz

pizarrón
blackboard
BLAHK-bord

pizarrón blanco
whiteboard
WAYT-bord

plátano
banana
buh-NAH-nuh

plato
plate
pleyt

playera
T-shirt
TI-shuhrt

polilla
moth
math

portería
goal
gol

postre
dessert
dih-ZUHRT

primo
cousin
KUH-zihn

puerro
leek
lik

puerta
door
dor

pulpo
octopus
AK-tuh-puhs

pulsera
bracelet
BREYS-liht

Q

queso
cheese
chiz

quince
fifteen
fihf-TIN

R

rábano
radish
RAH-dihsh

rana
frog
frag

raqueta de tenis
tennis racket
TEHN-ihs RAH-kiht

ratón
mouse
maus

rectángulo
rectangle
REHK-teyng-guhl

red
net
neht

refresco
soda
SO-duh

refrigerador
refrigerator
rih-FRIHJ-uhr-ey-duhr

regla
ruler
RU-luhr

reloj
clock
klak

remo
rowing
RO-ihng

rinoceronte
rhinoceros
ray-NA-suhr-ihs

rodilla
knee
ni

rojo
red
rehd

rombo
diamond
DAY-mihnd

ropa interior
underwear
UHN-duhr-wehr

rosa
pink
pihngk

S

sal
salt
salt

salmón
salmon
SAHM-uhn

saltamontes
grasshopper
GRAHS-ha-puhr

salto
diving
DAY-vihng

sandalias
sandals
SAHN-duhlz

sandía
watermelon
WA-duhr-mehl-uhn

sándwich
sandwich
SAHND-wihch

sartén
pan
pahn

secadora
dryer
DRAY-uhr

secadora de cabello
hair dryer
HEHR-dray-uhr

seis
six
sihks

senderismo
hiking
HAY-kihng

serpiente
snake
sneyk

servilleta
napkin
NAHP-kihn

sesenta
sixty
SIHKS-di

setenta
seventy
SEH-vuhn-di

short
shorts
shorts

siete
seven
SEH-vihn

silla
chair
chehr

sobrina
niece
nis

sobrino
nephew
NEH-fyu

sofá
couch
kauch

sombrero
hat
haht

sopa
soup
sup

sótano
basement
BEYS-mihnt

soya
soybean
SOY-bin

suéter
sweater
SWEH-duhr

surf
surfing
SUHR-fihng

T

tacones
high heels
hay hilz

talón
heel
hil

taxi
taxi
TAHK-si

taza
cup
kuhp

té
tea
ti

techo
roof
ruf

televisión
television
TEH-luh-vih-zhihn

tenedor
fork
fork

tenis (calzado)
sneakers
SNI-kurz

tenis (deporte)
tennis
TEH-nihs

tenis de mesa
table tennis
TEY-buhl TEHN-ihs

tetera
tea kettle
ti KEH-duhl

tía
aunt
ahnt

tiburón
shark
shark

tigre
tiger
TAY-guhr

tijeras
scissors
SIH-zuhrz

tío
uncle
UHNG-kuhl

toalla
towel
TAU-uhl

Lista de vocabulario

tobillo
ankle
AHNG-kuhl

tomate
tomato
tuh-MEY-do

topo
mole
mol

toronja
grapefruit
GREYP-frut

tortuga
turtle
TUHR-duhl

tostador
toaster
TOS-duhr

traje
suit
sut

traje de baño
bathing suit
BEY-thihng sut

trece
thirteen
thuhr-TIN

treinta
thirty
THUHR-di

tren
train
treyn

tres
three
thri

triángulo
triangle
TRAY-ahng-guhl

trigo
wheat
wit

U

uña
fingernail
FIHNG-guhr-neyl

uña del pie
toenail
TO-neyl

uniforme
uniform
YU-nih-form

uno
one
wuhn

uvas
grapes
greyps

V

vaca
cow
kau

vajilla
dishes
DIH-shihz

vaso
glass
glahs

veinte
twenty
TWUHN-i

vela
sailing
SEYL-ihng

velero
sailboat
SEYL-bot

venado
deer
dihr

ventana
window
WIHN-do

ventilador
fan
fahn

verde
green
grin

vestido
dress
drehs

vinagre
vinegar
VIH-nuh-guhr

voleibol
volleyball
VA-li-bal

Y

yogur
yogurt
YO-guhrt

Z

zanahoria
carrot
KEH-riht

zanahoria blanca
parsnip
PAR-snihp

zarzamora
blackberry
BLAHK-beh-ri

zorrillo
skunk
skuhngk

zorro
fox
faks